THE HUS
FAN

First Edition

By Tim Murphy

Copyright 2015
Shamrock Arrow Media

For information on Tim Murphy's other cookbook releases visit www.flanneljohn.com

THE HUSKIES FOOTBALL FAN COOKBOOK

TABLE OF CONTENTS

APPETIZERS & SNACKS

BEER CHEESE SOUP

3 slices of bacon, cut into quarters
½ cup of green onion, chopped
2 tablespoons of flour
1 can of cream of chicken soup
2 cups of shredded cheddar cheese
1 can of beer
1 cup of milk

Cook bacon until crisp. Add onion and sauté until tender. Remove from heat and stir in flour. Add in the chicken soup and bring to a boil. Stir in the shredded cheddar cheese until melted. Stir in beer and milk until foam disappears and soup is not. Don't let the soup boil.

BLITZED BAKED BEANS

2 cans pork and beans
1½ cups brown sugar
½ cup butter
¼ teaspoon hickory seasoning

Drain beans and remove pork lard. Mix ingredients in bowl and bake at 250 degrees for 3 hours.

BOLOGNA BALL

2 pounds of bologna
  (ring or whole, not sliced)
1 green pepper
2 eggs, hard-boiled
½ onion, small
½ cup of relish
Miracle Whip
Nuts, chopped

Grind bologna, pepper, eggs, onion and relish together. Form into a large ball, cover with Miracle Whip and roll in nuts.

CHEESE PUFFS

2 cups of cheddar cheese, shredded
1¼ cups of flour
½ cup of margarine
24 olives

Mix flour and cheese with melted margarine. With the dough, form it around each olive. Put the wrapped olives on a cookie sheet. Bake at 400 degrees for 15 to 20 minutes.

CHEESE STRAWS

1 cup of flour
½ cup of cheddar cheese, grated or shredded
½ teaspoon of salt
1/3 cup of shortening
3 tablespoons of water

Mix flour salt, cheese and shortening. Add water. Roll very thin and cut into strips. Put on a greased cookie sheet and bake at 425 degrees for 10 minutes.

CHINESE MEATBALLS

1½ pounds ground beef
½ cup rice, washed
1 teaspoon of salt
½ teaspoon pepper
1 tablespoon of onion, minced
1 small can tomato soup

Combine beef, rice, salt, pepper and onion, shape into small balls. Heat tomato soup with ½ cup of water in a pan. Drop meatballs into soup mixture and cover. Simmer for one hour.

FIRE & ICE SALSA

3 cups of seeded and chopped watermelon
½ cup of green pepper, chopped
2 tablespoons of lime juice
1 tablespoon of cilantro
3 jalapenos, seeded and minced
½ teaspoon of garlic salt

Mix ingredients, cover and refrigerate for 4 hours.

FIRST & TEN SAUSAGE BALLS

2 pounds of sausage (chopped or diced)
3 cups of Bisquick
1 large jar of Cheez Whiz

Mix all ingredients in a bowl. Form into 1-inch balls and bake at 350 degrees for 15 minutes.

GOLDEN NUGGETS CHICKEN

3 to 4 chicken breasts
1 cup of breadcrumbs
½ Parmesan cheese
1 teaspoon of thyme
1 teaspoon of basil
½ teaspoon salt
¾ cup margarine

Cut chicken into nuggets. Melt margarine. Mix remaining ingredients together. Dip chicken into margarine then bread crumb mixture. Place on cookie sheet, bake at 350 degrees for 45 minutes.

GRANOLA BARS

½ cup corn syrup
½ cup peanut butter
2 cups granola cereal
¼ cup raisins
¼ cup peanuts (or nut of choice)

Combine granola, raisins and nuts and mix well. Heat corn syrup to a boil and blend in peanut butter. Immediately pour over granola mixture and mix quickly to coat. Press firmly into an 8-inch square pan. Cool before cutting into bars.

HOMEFIELD POTATO CHIPS

3 large potatoes
Vegetable oil
Salt

Slice potatoes paper thin to about one-sixteenth of an inch. Place slices in ice water until you are ready to fry. In a deep fryer or pan, heat oil to 375 degrees. Place 6 to 8 slices on paper towels to dry then slide slices one at a time into the oil. Fry 8 slices at a time until golden brown. Drain on paper towel and salt. You can also try celery or garlic salt.

KITCHEN SINK TRAIL MIX

½ cup of banana chips
1 cup of Rice Chex
¼ cup of chocolate or vanilla chips
½ cup of raisins or craisins
1 cup of mini pretzels
1 cup of Cheerios
¼ cup of cashews
¼ cup of almond slivers
½ cup of dried apple
¼ cup of dried apricot

Put all ingredients in a paper bag and shake thoroughly. Pour into a bowl and serve. Measurements are just an example, adjust ingredients to taste.

LOCKER ROOM GORP

Raisins
Dry roasted peanuts or almonds
Sunflower seeds, shelled
Rolled Oats
M&Ms, carob, chocolate or vanilla chips

Mix equal parts of each ingredient and store in a sealed container or plastic bag.

LONG BOMB NACHOS

2 green onions, diced
½ bag of tortilla chips
1 cup of cheese, shredded
2 ounces of olives, sliced
2 tablespoons of sour cream
1 can of refried beans
Salsa

Pour chips in a baking dish. Spread refried beans evenly over the chips and sprinkle with grated cheese. Bake mixture at 350 degrees for 10 to 15 minutes or until cheese is melted. When it's time to serve top with salsa, olives green onions and sour cream.

O-LINE BEANS & HAM HOCKS

1 package of white beans
1 large can of tomatoes
1 onion, diced
½ pound of brown sugar
2 ham hocks

Soak beans overnight in water then boil for 20 minutes. Pour off the liquid. Put beans and remaining ingredients in a covered baking dish. Bake at 300 degrees for 5 to 6 hours. If needed, add a little water occasionally. Makes enough for 10 kickers or 2 centers.

OVER-STUFFED JALAPENOS

¼ pound of ground beef
12 popper-size jalapeños
1 small onion, diced
1 pound of bacon
14 ounces Monterey Jack with jalapeños
Cooking oil

In a skillet, brown onion in oil. Add hamburger, brown and drain. Grate cheese and mix with hamburger. Cut top of jalapeños and core out the seeds. Slit down to ¼ inch from bottom. Stuff peppers with hamburger mixture. Wrap slice of bacon around popper. Stick with toothpick. Bake, broil or grill.

POWER SWEEP WRAPS

1 package of dry salami slices
1 can of chopped olives
1 carton of whipped cream cheese
Toothpicks

Mix cream cheese and chopped olives to your taste. Spread the mixture lightly in a salami piece. Roll up the salami and secure with a toothpick.

PRETZEL DEVILS

1½ pounds of pretzels (sticks, chunks, etc.)
1 teaspoon of cayenne pepper
1 teaspoon of lemon pepper
1 teaspoon of garlic powder
1 package of dry ranch dressing mix
½ cup of canola oil
Large Ziploc bag or small garbage bag

Mix all ingredients, except pretzels, in a bowl. Take a bag of pretzels and empty it into a plastic bag. Be careful not to pour in the excess salt from the pretzel bag. Slowly pour dry ingredients over pretzels and seal up the bag. Shake vigorously until all pretzels are coated. Pour seasoned pretzels into a roasting pan. Bake at 250 degrees for 1 hour then serve.

RED DOG CHICKEN CHUNKS

4 chicken breasts, boneless & skinless
1 bottle of ranch dressing
Crushed cornflakes
Red pepper flakes (optional)

Crush corn flakes in a bowl. Pour dressing in a second bowl. Cut chicken breasts into chunks. Dip chicken into dressing and then roll in cornflakes. For an extra kick, combine pepper flakes with corn flakes. Put the chicken chunks on a cookie sheet. Bake at 375 degrees for 7 to 9 minutes.

SOFT PRETZELS

3½ cups of flour
1½ cups of warm water
1 tablespoon of yeast
1 tablespoon of sugar
Coarse salt

Mix water, yeast and sugar. Add flour gradually until a dough ball forms. Dough should be workable but not sticky. Don't over knead. Put some oil on your hands so dough won't cling to your hands. Divide dough in half, then in quarters. Make 3 dough balls from each quarter. Roll each ball into a rope then twist into a pretzel. Place on a baking sheet and sprinkle with salt. Bake for 12 to 15 minutes.

STUFFED
(AT THE LINE OF SCRIMMAGE)
PEPPERS

1 can of chili, no beans
4 bell peppers
1 can of corn, drained
Tortilla chips
Hot sauce (optional)

Cut the tops of the peppers and remove the insides. Boil in water for 12 to 15 minutes and drain. In a pan combine chili and corn and heat until cooked. Fill peppers with the mixture and hot sauce. Serve peppers with chips.

SWEDISH MEATBALLS

¾ cup of breadcrumbs
½ pound of ground veal
2 pounds of ground beef
¼ pound of ground pork
2 eggs
3 teaspoons of salt
2 onions, chopped
¼ cup of parsley
Pepper to taste
Water

Add water to breadcrumbs to form a damp paste. Mix with remaining ingredients. Refrigerate until cool. Form into 1½-inch balls and slowly brown in a skillet.

TRAIL MIX

2 cups of salted peanuts
1 cup of raisins
1 cup of dried cranberries
1 cup of almond slivers
1 cup of M&M candies

Mix ingredients. That's it. Now get back to the beer.

BURGERS

BBQ PORK BURGERS

2 pounds of ground pork
¼ cup fresh breadcrumbs
1 cup of barbecue sauce
6 burger buns
Salt and pepper (optional)

Mix ground pork with breadcrumbs and ½ cup of sauce to make six patties. Grill burgers on medium high heat, basting burgers often with remaining sauce. Takes about 10 minutes to cook, 5 per side.

BLACK & BLEU CHEESE BURGERS

2 pounds of ground beef
8 ounces crumbled blue cheese
2 tablespoons onion powder
2 tablespoons garlic powder
2 tablespoons soy sauce
2 teaspoons salt
4 slices Swiss cheese
4 hamburger buns

Combine beef, bleu cheese, onion powder, garlic powder, soy sauce and salt in a bowl. Mix well. Make 4 large patties. Grill patties on high heat for about 8 minutes per side or until well done. Top with Swiss cheese

CLAM BURGERS

1 pint of razor clam necks, uncooked
2 eggs
1 teaspoon of parsley flakes
2½ teaspoons of onion flakes
4 drops of Tabasco or hot sauce of choice
2 teaspoons of Worcestershire sauce
¼ teaspoon of pepper
1 teaspoon of biscuit mix
3 soda crackers
Butter
Hamburger buns

Grind clams. Beat eggs and add parsley flakes, dried onion flakes, Tabasco, Worcestershire sauce, pepper and biscuit mix. Crumble soda crackers and add all of these ingredients to ground, mixed clams and mix well. Form small patties and fry in ½ to 1-inch of oil in a pan. Brown both sides well. Check center for doneness. Serve on buttered, toasted buns.

CRAB BURGERS

8 hamburger buns (day old if possible)
2 cups of crabmeat
1 cup of shredded sharp cheddar cheese
1 to 1½ cups of mayonnaise
1 teaspoon of lemon juice
Garlic powder to taste

Mix all ingredients. Place mixture on hamburger buns and bake in the oven at 350 degrees until the cheese is bubbly.

HOBO HAMBURGER

1 pound of hamburger
1 onion
2 carrots
2 potatoes
Salt and pepper to taste

Make burger patties and place on aluminum foil. Thinly slice onions, carrots and potatoes and place on top of meat. Salt and pepper to taste. Fold foil into a pocket and fold edges over. Cook on grill or open fire.

JAMAICAN JERK TURKEY BURGERS

1 teaspoon of salt
1 tablespoon of pepper
1 tablespoon of thyme
4 teaspoons of allspice
1 habanero pepper, minced
4 scallions, chopped
1 pound of ground turkey
4 slices of Muenster cheese
1 onion, sliced
1 tomato, sliced
1 mango, peeled and sliced

Mix spices, habanero and scallions together to make the jerk seasoning. Mix ¼ cup of the seasoning with the ground turkey. Save remainder for future use. Make 4 patties from the meat. Grill on a barbecue or in a frying pan. Put burgers on buns and top with cheese, onion, tomato and mango.

NOT-SO-SLOPPY-JOE BBQ BURGERS

1 pound of ground beef
1 cup chopped onion
1 cup of ketchup
2 tablespoons mustard
1 teaspoon of salt
1 teaspoon of sugar
1 teaspoon of vinegar
½ teaspoon cloves (optional)

Brown ground beef and onions. Stir in remaining ingredients. Cover and simmer 30 minutes. Optional method: form 4 to 6 patties with all ingredients and toss them on the grill.

ONION BURGERS

1 pound of ground beef
1 cup of chopped celery
1 can of condensed French Onion soup
¼ cup of water
¼ cup of catsup
1 teaspoon of Worcestershire sauce
1 teaspoon of yellow mustard
¼ teaspoon of pepper
Hamburger buns

Brown ground beef and celery in a pan and pour off fat. Add remaining ingredients and cook over low heat for 12 to 15 minutes. Scoop onto buns.

OVER-STUFFED BURGERS

2 pounds of ground beef
3 eggs
1½ teaspoons of flour
1 onion, finely diced
1 tablespoon of salt
¼ teaspoon of pepper
2 cups of mushrooms
¼ cup butter
8 slices of bacon

Mix meat, eggs, flour, onion, salt and pepper. Roll out on a cookie sheet. Cut into 16 thin, square patties. Sauté the mushrooms in butter and top 8 of the patties. Cut each bacon strip in half and place on top of the mushrooms. Now place the remaining patties on top, pinching the edges, creating the "over-stuffed" burger. Broil, grill or bake the patties for 8 to 12 minutes. Depending on how you like it, you can fry the bacon before you put it in the burger.

PORCELAIN PALACE MINI-BURGERS

1½ pounds of ground beef
1 egg
1 instant onion soup mix
½ cup diced onion
2 teaspoons water

Mix and press into a cookie sheet. Poke holes in meat placing diced onions in holes. Bake at 400 degrees for 10 minutes. Cut into squares use dinner rolls for buns.

TERIYAKI BURGERS

1 pound of ground beef
3 tablespoons of sake or dry sherry
1 teaspoon of sugar
3 tablespoons of soy sauce
2 cloves of garlic, minced
½ teaspoon of ginger, ground
4 buns

Combine all ingredients thoroughly and form into 4 patties. Barbecue or grill 4 to 5 per side.

TUNA BURGERS

1 can of tuna fish
1 egg
½ cup of cracker crumbs
¼ cup of milk
¼ teaspoon of onion flakes
¼ teaspoon of oregano
Salt and pepper to taste
Cheddar cheese
Tomato slices
Lettuce
Oil

Mix fish, egg, cracker crumbs, milk, onion, oregano, salt and pepper then form into patties. Fry in skillet. Top with cheese, tomato and lettuce and serve on buttered, toasted hamburger buns.

TURKEY BURGERS

1 pound of fresh ground turkey
¼ cup of chili sauce
1 teaspoon of chicken flavor bouillon powder

Combine all of the ingredients, shape into patties and grill.

CHICKEN
WINGS

CAJUN WINGS

2 pounds of chicken wings
1 tablespoon of vegetable oil
1 teaspoon of crushed red pepper
2 teaspoons of Cajun seasoning
¾ teaspoon of corn flour
6 tablespoons of brown sugar
2 cups of orange juice
1½ cups of lemon juice

Combine vegetable oil, red pepper, Cajun seasoning, chili powder, corn flour and brown sugar in a bowl and mix well. Stir in orange and lemon juices. Place chicken wings in a dish and cover with mixture, holding back ½ cup. Cover the dish and place in refrigerator overnight. Remove from the refrigerator and place coated wings in a baking dish. Bake at 300 degrees for 20 to 25 minutes, basting every few minutes with the extra half-cup of sauce.

C.C. CHICKEN WINGS

2 pounds of chicken wings
1 12-ounce can of cola (or cherry cola)
1 cup of ketchup
1 tablespoon Worcestershire (optional)

Place wings in a pan. Mix the ingredients thoroughly and pour over wings. Cook at 375 degrees for about 60 minutes while occasionally basting to keep wings glazed.

EAST VS. WEST WINGS

3 pounds of chicken wings
1 cup of soy sauce
1 cup of sugar
¼ cup of vinegar
¼ teaspoon of ginger

Place the chicken wings in a large baking dish. Mix remaining ingredients together and pour sauce over wing. Bake at 325 degrees for two hours. Baste occasionally.

FULL ROSTER WINGS

2 dozen chicken wings
1 cup of pineapple juice
1 cup of soy sauce
1 cup of sugar
¼ cup of water
¼ cup of vegetable oil
2 cloves garlic, crushed
1 teaspoon of ginger

Combine all ingredients in pan except chicken and ginger. Once thoroughly combined, add ginger and refrigerate overnight. Next day, pour off about 1 cup of liquid and place chicken in the pan. Bake uncovered at 350 degrees for 60 minutes. Baste wings with remaining liquid during baking.

HUSKY WINGS

3 pounds of chicken wings
½ cup of soy sauce
½ cup of coconut syrup
½ of thawed frozen orange juice concentrate

Cut through each full wing to make two pieces, Line a baking sheet with foil. Combine ingredients and pour half over chicken. Bake at 400 degrees for 15 to 20 minutes. Turn chicken and pour remaining sauce over chicken. Bake for another 15 to minutes.

SESAME WINGS

2 dozen chicken wings
½ cup of flour
½ cup of cornstarch
1 teaspoon of salt
½ cup of brown sugar
2 eggs
5 tablespoons of soy sauce
2 cloves of garlic, minced

Combine flour, cornstarch, salt, sugar, eggs, soy sauce and garlic. Marinate wings in sauce overnight in a refrigerator. Put wings on a cookie sheet and bake at 350 degrees for 20 to 30 minutes.

STADIUM WINGS

10 Chicken wings
½ cup of melted margarine
1 small box of Parmesan cheese
1 teaspoon of garlic powder

Dip chicken wings in margarine. Combine cheese and garlic powder. Coat wings with the mixture and place on a cookie sheet. Bake at 350 degrees for 1 hour.

WASHINGTON WINGS

1 pound of chicken wings
1 package of dry French onion soup mix
8 ounces of Russian dressing
12 ounces of apricot preserves

In a single layer, spread wings in a large baking dish. In a pan, mix soup, dressing and preserves and bring to a boil while stirring constantly. Reduce heat and simmer for 5 minutes. Pour sauce over chicken. Bake uncovered at 350 degrees for 1 hour.

CHILI & CHOWDER

CHICKEN CHILI

1 pound of boneless skinless chicken, diced
3 cups of chicken broth or stock
1½ cups of diced tomatoes with juice
2 jalapenos chopped with seeds removed
15 ounces of pinto or red beans (canned)
15 ounces of black beans (canned)
2 tablespoons of oil
1 medium onion, chopped
2 large cloves of garlic, minced
4 teaspoons of chili powder
1 tablespoon of ground cumin
2 teaspoons of oregano
Lime and cilantro (optional)

Drain and rinse beans. Sauté onion and garlic in oil. Add chicken and cook on medium until meat is no longer pink. Stir in chili powder, cumin and oregano. Add chicken stock, tomatoes, jalapenos, salt, pepper and beans. Simmer uncovered.

FIRST AND GOAL CHILI

1 pound of meat (venison, beef, mountain
   goat, squirrel, etc.)
2 cans of stewed tomatoes
4 cans of pinto chili beans
1 green pepper
1 onion, diced
1 teaspoon of chili powder
Salt and pepper

Brown meat and sprinkle with salt, pepper and chili powder. Combine with beans and stewed tomatoes. Chop onion and green pepper and stir-fry in meat grease until tender. Pour into bean mixture and simmer for 30 minutes.

I-5 CHILI

2 pounds of ground beef
1 cup of onion, chopped
1 clove of garlic, minced
1½ teaspoons of salt
1 teaspoon of paprika
1 teaspoon of oregano
1/3 cup of chili powder
15 ounces of tomato sauce
16 ounces of pinto beans
2 cups of water

Brown ground beef with onion, garlic and seasonings. Add tomato sauce, water and pinto beans. Simmer for at least one hour. Start making it just before kick-off and it will be ready at half time.

LINEBACKER BLITZ CHILI

2 pounds of ground chuck
1 cup of onion, chopped
1 clove of garlic, chopped
1½ teaspoons of salt
1 teaspoon of paprika
1 teaspoon of oregano
¼ cup of chili powder
15 ounces of tomato sauce
2 cups of water
16 ounces of canned pinto beans

Brown the meat in a pot with onion, garlic and seasonings. Add in the tomato sauce, water and pinto beans. Simmer for 60 to 75 minutes. For more heat add in an additional tablespoon or two of chili powder or hot sauce.

RAZOR CLAM CHOWDER

1 pint of razor clams with liquid
1 quart of milk
4 potatoes, diced
1 onion, finely diced
4 sliced of bacon, diced
Salt and pepper to taste

Fry bacon until golden brown and drain the grease. Add the bacon to the clams. In a pot, brown onion slightly then add clams, bacon and potatoes. Cover with water and simmer until potatoes are cooked. Pour in milk and season to taste. Heat until piping hot but not boiling.

SALMON CHOWDER

2 pounds of salmon, canned or fresh
15 ounces of creamed corn
12 ounces of evaporated milk
8 ounces of cheddar cheese, shredded
2 cups of potatoes, diced
2 cups of chicken broth
2 carrots, diced
¾ cup of onion, diced
½ cup of celery, diced
3 tablespoons of butter
1 teaspoon of garlic powder
1 teaspoon of salt
1 teaspoon of pepper
1 teaspoon of dill

Melt butter in a large pot. Sauté onion, celery and garlic powder over medium heat until onions are tender. Stir in broth, potatoes, carrots, salt, pepper and dill. Bring to a boil and reduce heat. Cover and simmer for 20 minutes. Cut salmon into pieces or flakes. Add the salmon, evaporated milk, corn and cheese. Cook until thoroughly heated.

TRAINING ROOM CHILI

1 pound of ground beef
1 cup of chopped onion
2 cans of tomato sauce
2 cans of pinto beans
1 can of diced tomatoes
2 cloves of garlic, diced
2 tablespoons of chili powder
Salt and pepper to taste

Brown beef, onions and garlic then drain and return to pan. Add tomato sauce and tomatoes. Drain beans and add to mixture. Stir in chili powder and salt and pepper to taste. Simmer on low heat for 30 minutes.

DESSERTS

APPLE CUP CAKE

3 cups of peeled, chopped red apple
3 cups of flour
2 cups of sugar
1 teaspoon of cinnamon
1 teaspoon of salt
1 teaspoon of baking soda
2 teaspoons of vanilla
2 eggs, beaten
1 cup of oil

Mix all ingredients and pour into a greased and floured pan. Bake at 350 degrees for 1 hour.

APPLE CUP CRISP

5 cups of sliced apples
¾ cup of flour
1 teaspoon of cinnamon
1 cup of brown sugar
¾ cup of rolled oats
½ cup of butter

Arrange apples in a buttered pan. Combine sugar, flour, oats and cinnamon. Cut in butter until crumbly. Press over apples. Bake at 350 degrees for about 45 minutes.

ARMY NAVY DOUGHNUTS

5 cups flour
2 cups sugar
½ teaspoon salt
1 teaspoon of nutmeg
2 eggs
5 teaspoons baking powder
1¼ cups of milk
1 teaspoon melted butter

Sift dry ingredients. Combine eggs, butter and milk. Add dry ingredients. Mix well. Shape into a ball and knead. Roll out on floured surface and cut with doughnut cutter. Place in deep fryer or in a deep skillet. Makes four dozen. This recipe was used to serve tens of thousands of allied troops throughout Europe during World War I.

BELL RUNG COOKIES
(Set 'em and forget 'em)

2 egg whites
¾ cup of sugar
¼ teaspoon of salt
1 teaspoon of vanilla
6 ounces of chocolate chips

Beat eggs whites until stiff. Gradually fold in sugar and salt and continue beating. Fold in chocolate chips. Drop by teaspoon onto a greased cookie sheet. Place in an oven heated to 350 degrees and immediately turn off oven. Leave the cookies in the oven overnight.

BLACK & WHITE PEANUTS

1 large package of milk chocolate chips
1 large package of vanilla chips
16 ounces of unsalted, dry roasted peanuts

Combine the two packages of chips. Microwave on high for 2½ to 3 minutes or melt in a double boiler or in a small pan in a larger pan of water. Add peanuts. Microwave for another 2 minutes or 4 minutes in pan while stirring. Drop spoonfuls on an ungreased cookie sheet. Refrigerate for one hour.

CRACK BACK
CHOCOLATE CHIP COOKIES

¾ cup of butter flavored Crisco
1¼ cup of firmly packed brown sugar
1 egg
2 tablespoons of milk
1 tablespoon of vanilla extract
1¾ cups of flour
1 teaspoon of salt
¾ teaspoon of soda
1 cup of semisweet chocolate chips
1 cup of pecan pieces (optional)

Mix ingredients well and place on a cookie sheet. Bake at 375 degrees for 8 to 10 minutes. If not using nuts, add an extra ½ cup of chocolate chips.

DOWN MARKER OREO BALLS

1 package of Oreos
8 ounces of cream cheese
7 ounces of Bakers Dipping Chocolate
    (microwaveable)
Popsicle sticks or skewers

Crush Oreo cookies. Add cream cheese and roll into 1½-inch balls. Insert sticks into balls and dip into melted chocolate. Freeze or refrigerate until hard. Dip balls a second time and place back in the refrigerator. Serve "down markers" on green florist foam to look like turf.

END ZONE SPIKED BALLS

2½ cups of vanilla wafer crumbs
3 tablespoons of white Karo syrup
3 tablespoons of cocoa powder
4½ ounces of rum or whiskey
1 cup of chopped nuts
Powdered sugar

Mix all ingredients together except powdered sugar. Form into balls slightly smaller than a golf ball. Roll in powdered sugar and let stand overnight to dry. Store in an airtight container.

FOOTBALL DRAFT COOKIES

Guys, you can pull these off. It's three ingredients, but don't burn the chips! Keep the heat low.

> 6 ounces of butterscotch chips
> 12 ounces of chocolate chips
> 1 large package of chow mien noodles

Melt chips together and stir in noodles thoroughly. Drop cookies on wax paper with a spoon and cool.

GRIDIRON SQUARES

3 cups of cornflakes
1 cup of white Karo syrup
1 cup of sugar
1 cup of peanut butter
Butter

Mix Karo syrup and sugar in a pan over low heat then slowly bring to a boil. Stir in peanut butter, remove from heat and mix well. Pour into a buttered 9-inch by 13-inch pan. Let cool and cut into squares.

KAHLUA BOWL CAKE

1 box of chocolate cake mix
1 pint of sour cream
¼ cup of Kahlua
2 eggs
1/3 cup of vegetable oil
6 ounces of chocolate chips

Mix the dry cake mix thoroughly with the other ingredients. Because brands differ, follow baking directions on the box.

PEANUT BRITTLE

1 cup of molasses
½ cup of melted butter
1 cup of peanuts

Heat molasses and butter until well cooked; stir in peanuts and continue boiling until candy is brittle when tested with cold water. Pour into a shallow, well-greased or buttered pan. Cut into squares and let cool.

SEA MONSTER COOKIES

1 cup of butter or margarine
1 pound of brown sugar
2 cups of sugar
6 eggs
1½ teaspoons of vanilla extract
1½ teaspoons of syrup
4 teaspoons of baking soda
1½ pounds of peanut butter
9 cups of uncooked rolled oats
1 pound of M&Ms
6 ounces of chocolate chips

Mix ingredients in the order listed. Drop tablespoons of the mixture on a greased cookie sheet. Flatten a bit. Bake at 350 degrees for 12 minutes.

THREE POINT STANCE PB FUDGE

¼ cup of honey
½ cup of peanut butter
¾ cup of powdered milk

Mix the three ingredients together. Spoon and smooth into an 8-inch by 8-inch pan. Chill overnight. Cut into 9 squares.

WIDE OUT BARS

1 cup of softened butter
1 cup of dark brown sugar
1 egg yolk
2 teaspoons of vanilla
2 cups of flour
¼ teaspoon of salt
6 ounces of chocolate chips

Cream butter and sugar together until fluffy. Add in egg yolk and vanilla and beat until smooth. Now add in salt and flour and mix until thoroughly blended. Press the dough into a 9-inch by 13-inch baking dish. Bake at 350 degrees for 15 to 20 minutes. It should be light brown and soft to the touch. Remove from oven and immediately sprinkle with chocolate chips. Let rest for a few minutes and evenly spread melted chocolate with a knife. Let rest for a few minutes and cut into squares.

WOODY'S BUCKEYES

1 package of graham crackers, crushed
2¾ cups of powdered sugar
1 cup of peanut butter (crunchy or smooth)
1 cup of butter, melted
Chocolate or chocolate chips, melted

Combine crumbs and sugar. Melt butter and peanut butter then add to crumb mixture. Form into balls about 1½-inches in diameter. Chill, dip into melted chocolate and chill again.

DIPS

ARTICHOKE DIP

1 small can of artichoke hearts, chopped
2 tablespoons of green onion, chopped
1 cup of mayonnaise
1 cup of Parmesan cheese

Mix all ingredients in a baking dish. Bake at 325 degrees for 20 minutes.

BAR CHEESE

2 pounds of Velveeta cheese
6 ounces of horseradish
8 drops of Tabasco sauce
1 cup of mayonnaise

Combine cheese, Tabasco sauce and horseradish in a double boiler. If you don't have a double boiler, put ingredients in a small pot and place in a larger pot half-filled with water. Once melted, remove from heat and add mayonnaise. Mix thoroughly. Pour into a container and let cool.

BLACK BEAN DIP

15 ounces of black beans (canned)
2 ounces of black olive pieces
1 teaspoon of taco seasoning
½ cup of salsa
½ cup of ranch dressing
3 scallions, diced
1 tomato, diced

Combine all ingredients and mix well. Serve with corn chips.

CHILI DIP

8 ounces of cream cheese
1 can of chili (no beans)
½ cup of grated cheddar cheese

Place cream cheese in the bottom of a microwaveable baking dish. Cover with chili and top with grated cheese. Heat in the microwave on high for 3 minutes or until cheese melts.

CHILI CHEESE DIP

1 green pepper, chopped
1 onion, chopped
2 tablespoons butter
15 ounces of chili (no beans)
1 can cream of mushroom soup
¼ teaspoon garlic powder
1 pound of sharp cheddar cheese, grated
Corn chips

Sauté pepper and onion. Add no-beans chili, soup and garlic then simmer. Add cheese before serving. Make a great hot dog topping too.

CLAM DIP

16 ounces of softened cream cheese
1 can of clams with juice
2 green onions, finely diced
3 dashes of Worcestershire sauce
Salt and pepper to taste

Mix all the ingredients together. Serve with vegetable sticks or chips.

CRAB DIP

16 ounces of cream cheese
2 tablespoons of chopped onion
1 teaspoon of horseradish
1 teaspoon of Worcestershire sauce
2 drops of Tabasco sauce
1 pound of crab (fresh or frozen)

Let seafood thaw and drain/. Let cream cheese soften to room temperature. Combine all ingredients in a baking dish. Bake at 325 degrees for 20 to 25 minutes.

MANGO SALSA

½ red onion, diced
½ bunch of cilantro, finely chopped
2 mangos, peeled, seeded and diced
Juice from 1 lime
Salt and pepper to taste

Mix ingredients together and enjoy. Works great as a dip or with fish.

SEVEN BLOCKS OF GRANITE DIP

2 cans of refried beans
20 ounces of jalapeno bean dip
1 carton of avocado dip
1 cup of sour cream
1 package of taco seasoning mix
2 tomatoes, diced
2 cups of cheddar cheese, shredded
4 ounces of chopped black olives
1 cup of green onion, chopped

In a baking dish spread the bean dip followed by avocado dip. Combine sour cream and taco seasoning for the third layer. Next, top in order with tomatoes, cheese, olives and onions.

SHRIMP DIP

4 ounces of shrimp
½ cup of celery, chopped
½ cup of onion, diced
½ cup of mayonnaise
1 small package of cream cheese
1½ teaspoons of lemon juice

Chop shrimp into pieces. Mix with additional ingredients and chill for 3 hours in the refrigerator.

TWO-MINUTE WARNING GUACAMOLE

4 large avocados
¼ cup of cilantro, minced
2 cloves of garlic, minced
½ cup of salsa
Juice of one lime

Peel, pit and mash the avocados. Now add remaining ingredients and stir well. If you want a less chunky style, drop the ingredients in a blender.

DRINKS

BOWL SEASON EGG NOG

4 eggs, beaten
8 teaspoons of sugar
2 cups of cream
2 cups of milk
1 teaspoon of vanilla
Nutmeg

Whip eggs with a hand mixer or whisk. Add salt, sugar, milk, cream and vanilla. Whip entire mixture again. Finish with a dash of nutmeg.

CITRUS COOLER

¾ cup of sugar
1¼ cups of boiling water
3 cups of pineapple juice
3 cups of orange juice
¾ cup of lemon juice
2 liter bottle of cold ginger ale

Dissolve sugar in the boiling water. Mix fruit juices with sugar water and freeze until slushy. Remove from freezer and stir in ginger ale.

CHEERLEADERS PINK LEMONADE
MILKSHAKE

1½ cups of frozen pink lemonade
   concentrate
3 cups milk
10 scoops vanilla ice cream

Mix together in a blender. Makes five to six servings. Works with regular lemonade too.

FIRST STRING LEMONADE

6 lemons
1 cup of sugar
6 cups of water

Cut lemons in half and put them in a 2-quart pitcher. Cover with sugar. Bring water to a boil and pour over sugar and lemons. Keep stirring to dissolve sugar. After 30 minutes, squeeze the juice out of lemons. Refrigerate until cold.

FROSTY SIDELINES COFFEE

1 cup of hot chocolate mix
1 cup of non-dairy creamer
½ cup instant coffee
½ teaspoon cinnamon
¼ teaspoon nutmeg
½ to ¾ cup sugar

Mix hot chocolate, creamer, coffee, cinnamon and nutmeg in a blender. Add in sugar and blend well. Drop in 3 to 4 heaping teaspoons per mug and pour in hot water.

GANG TACKLE PUNCH

1 quart of softened vanilla ice cream
1 quart of softened lime sherbet
1 quart of milk
1 quart of ginger ale
6 ounces of frozen lemonade concentrate
6 ounces of frozen limeade concentrate
2 cups of water

In a punch bowl stir together milk, ice cream and sherbet. In a separate pitcher mix lemonade, limeade and water. Pour this mixture over the ice cream mixture. Add ginger ale and stir slightly.

GEORGIA PEACH PUNCH

4 peaches, peeled, pitted and quartered
½ cup of fine sugar
½ cup of brandy
7 cups of Rhine wine
1 quarts of club soda, chilled

Put peaches in a pitcher and sprinkle with sugar. Add brandy and stir well. Stir in wine, cover and chill for 3 hours. Stir in club soda just before serving.

ICE BOWL HOT BUTTERED RUM

1½ cup of dark rum
2½ cups of boiling water
4 tablespoons of butter
4 teaspoons of sugar
4 cinnamon sticks
Nutmeg

Stir sugar and rum together with a cinnamon stick until sugar has dissolved. Add water and butter. Pour into four mugs, dust with nutmeg and place a cinnamon stick in each one.

JULIUS OF ORANGE

3 ounces of frozen orange juice concentrate
½ cup of milk
½ cup of water
¼ cup of sugar
½ teaspoon of vanilla
6 ice cubes

Put all ingredients in a blender. Blend until smooth, about 30 to 40 seconds.

NOVEMBER TAILGATE
HOT CIDER PUNCH

1½ quarts of orange juice
4 cups of apple cider
½ cup of lemon juice
¼ stick of butter
1½ cups of sugar
2 cups of water
8 whole cloves
1 tablespoon of cinnamon
1 teaspoon of ginger

In a large pot combine water, sugar, cloves, cinnamon and ginger. Simmer for 10 minutes and strain. Stir in orange juice, apple cider, lemon juice and butter then reheat.

PRE-SEASON PUNCH

3 quarts of water
¾ cup of loose tea
2 cups of sugar
¾ cup of frozen lemonade concentrate,
    thawed
3 cups of pineapple juice
Mint sprigs

Boil 3 cups of water and pour over tea. Steep for 15 minutes and strain. Stir in sugar until dissolved. Add lemonade, pineapple juice, remaining water and several mint sprigs. Serve over ice.

HOT DOGS & SAUSAGES

BACON CHEESE BBQ DOGS

8 hot dogs
8 hot dog buns
8 slices of cheddar cheese
8 slices of bacon
½ cup of barbecue sauce
1 red onion, diced

Place the bacon in a deep skillet. Cook over medium-high heat until browned and drain on paper towels. In a separate pan or on a barbecue, grill hot dogs cook browned and fully cooked, or until done to your taste. Lightly toast or grill hot dog buns. Now place a slice of cheese and bacon on each roll. Add a hot dog and top each with 1 tablespoon barbeque sauce and red onion.

BBQ PARTY SAUSAGE

1 pound of smoked Polish sausage
1 can of whole mushrooms
½ bottle of KC Masterpiece Barbecue Sauce
   (or sauce brand of your choice)

Bake and drain sausage and cut into bite-size chunks. Combine all ingredients, warm and serve.

BEER BARREL BRATS

4 bratwursts
1-2 bottles of beer
8 slices of pumpernickel bread
Spicy brown mustard
Horseradish
Oil

Slowly simmer brats in a large skillet with beer for 10 to 15 minutes. Place on an oiled grill or in a second oiled skillet on low heat. Once they're browned, slice each brat down the middle and make a sandwich with the pumpernickel bread. Spread with spicy brown mustard and/or horseradish. To be authentic, use a Wisconsin or Pennsylvania beer. Newcastle Ale works great too!

CHICAGO DOG

Hot Dogs (all beef preferred)
Poppy Seed buns
Dill pickle spears
Cucumber spears
Tomato slices
Pickled peppers
Diced onion
Mustard (yellow)
Sweet relish (electric green if available)
Celery salt

Grill or boil the hot dogs. Use very soft, fresh buns or steam them if needed. Load up your dogs with all the ingredients saving the celery salt for last.

CONEY ISLAND HOT DOG SAUCE

½ pound of ground round
¼ cup of water
¼ cup of chopped onion
1 clove of garlic, minced
1 cup of seasoned tomato sauce
¾ teaspoon of chili powder
½ teaspoon of MSG
½ teaspoon of salt
Pinch of cumin

Brown meat slowly and thoroughly. Break with fork until crumbly. Add remaining ingredients, simmer uncovered for about 20 minutes.

DETROIT CONEY DOGS

4 natural casing hot dogs
4 hot dog buns, sliced
1 can of chili sauce without beans
1 onion, diced
4 tablespoons of mustard

Place hot dogs in a skillet or on a grill for 5 to 8 minutes. Lightly toast or grill the buns. Heat the chili sauce in a pan or microwave. Put the dogs in the buns and top with chili, onions and mustard.

DIABLO DOGS

1 package of hot dogs
1 can of jalapeno peppers
1 package of fresh carrots
1 onion, coarsely chopped
Corn chips

Cut hot dogs into bite-sized chunks. Pare and cut carrots to ¼-inch thick slices. Put all ingredients in a slow cooker and heat until juice is reduced by half. Serve with corn chips.

HEART ATTACK WEENIES

1 package of Hillshire Farms Lil Smokies
1 package of bacon
½ cup of brown sugar
Toothpicks

Cut bacon into pieces big enough to wrap around weenies and sugar with a toothpick. Top each one with ½ teaspoon of brown sugar. Put them on a cookies sheet and bake for 20 minutes at 400 degrees. When serving, keep a cardiologist's phone number handy just in case.

HOT DOG TACO

4 hot dogs, diced into small pieces
2 ounces of Monterey Jack or cheddar
  cheese
¼ to ½ cup of picante sauce
Jalapeno pepper diced (optional)
Green pepper diced (optional)
Flour tortillas (warmed)

Place the first five ingredients in a skillet. Warm over low heat until cheese is melted. Place mixture in a flour tortilla and roll up.

KIELBASA LASAGNA WRAPS

1 kielbasa sausage
4 lasagna noodles
1 jar of Prego Original spaghetti sauce
Cheddar cheese
Mozzarella cheese

Cut sausage into 4 pieces. Split lengthwise but not all the way through, and stuff with cheese. Wrap each piece in a cooked lasagna noodle. Place in a baking dish and cover with spaghetti sauce. Bake at 325 degrees for 30 minutes.

PAC WEST HOT DOGS

¼ cup of butter
1 sweet onion thinly sliced
4 ounces of cream cheese
4 hot dogs (salmon dogs optional)
4 hot dog buns
Spicy brown mustard
Sauerkraut

Slowly melt butter in a skillet over medium heat. Add onions, and cook for 15 minutes or until the onions have softened and turned brown. Warm cream cheese over low heat in a small pan until very soft. Grill hot dogs until fully cooked. Lightly toast hot dog buns on both sides. Spread warm cream cheese on toasted hot dog bun, add hot dog, top with onions, mustard and sauerkraut. Try using a salmon hot dog for an authentic Northwest flavor.

PARKING LOT DOGS

8 hot dog buns
8 hot dogs
½ cup of butter
2 tablespoons of mustard
2 tablespoons of Parmesan cheese
1 tablespoon finely chopped green pepper
1 tablespoon of chopped onion
1 16-ounce can of pork and beans

Cream butter and add in mustard, cheese, onion and green pepper. Open split buns, place on foil and spread mixture. Cut dogs in half and place on buns. Top with beans. Bake at 350 degrees for 12 to 15 minutes.

PIGS IN A BLANKET

24 cocktail franks or sausages
2¼ cups of flour
¾ cup of shortening
1 teaspoon of salt
Ice water

Sift flour and salt into a bowl. With a mixer, cut in shortening and just enough ice water to hold the dough together. Chill the dough for 3 to 4 hours in the refrigerator. Roll out the dough to one-eighth inch in thickness. Cut the dough into squares big enough to wrap each frank. Pinch the sides of the dough to secure around the frank. Place the wrapped pigs on a lightly greased baking sheet. Bake at 400 degrees for 15 to 20 minutes or until pastry has turned a light brown.

TROPICAL HOT DOGS & BEANS

2 pounds of canned of baked beans
½ cup of brown sugar
1 cup of pineapple chunks, drained
2 tablespoons of vinegar
1 teaspoon of dry mustard
2 teaspoons of onion flakes
8 hot dogs cut into 1-inch slices

Mix ingredients in a dish and bake at 375 degrees for 30 minutes.

WHISKEY DOGS

1 pound of hot dogs
¾ cup of chili sauce or ketchup
¼ cup of packed brown sugar
1 tablespoon of grated onion
2 tablespoons of lemon juice
3 ounces of whiskey or bourbon

In a saucepan, mix chili sauce or ketchup with brown sugar, onion, lemon juice and whiskey. Bring to a boil. Add hot dogs and simmer for 30 minutes. You can also cook these in a crock-pot.

MAIN DISHES

BACON CHEDDAR PIE

12 slices of bacon, fried and crumbled
1 cup shredded cheese, Swiss or cheddar
1/3 cup chopped onion
1 cup Bisquick
1/8 teaspoon of pepper
4 eggs
2 cups milk
¼ teaspoon salt

Lightly grease pie plate. Sprinkle bacon, cheese and onion in pie plate. Beat remaining ingredients until smooth. Pour evenly into pie plate. Bake at 400 degrees for 35 minutes. Let stand for 5 minutes before cutting.

BEER BOILED SHRIMP

2 pounds of cleaned, large raw shrimp
2 12-ounce cans of beer
2 tablespoons of crab boil seasoning
Pepper, lemon wedges and cocktail sauce

In a large pot bring beer and seasoning to a boil. Dump in shrimp and cover. Return to a boil and simmer for five minutes. Turn off heat and leave shrimp in the pot for three minutes. Drain shrimp and serve with lemon wedges and cocktail sauce.

BEEFED-UP STEW

2 pounds of beef cut into 1-inch cubes
5 carrots cut into 1-inch slices
1 large onion, diced
3 stalks of celery, diced
1 quart of canned tomatoes or tomato juice
½ cup of quick cooking tapioca
½ teaspoon of ground clove
1 bay leaf
Salt and pepper to taste

Trim fat from beef. Put ingredients in a crock-pot. Cover and turn on high. Once it starts to cook, turn to low and cook 4 to 5 hours. Remove bay leaf.

CHILI CHEESE PIE

1 pie crust (top and bottom)
3 cups of chili
1 pound of cooked ground beef
1 cup of grated cheddar cheese
1 cup of corn chips

Place bottom crust in a 9-inch round pan. Cook ground beef and add chili. Pour mixture into pan and add grated cheese. Top with corn chips. Cover with top crust and cut holes into top crust. Bake at 350 degrees for 15 to 20 minutes until golden brown.

CROCKED BEEF STEW

3 pound of beef cut into 1½-inch chunks
2 cans of cream of mushroom soup
¾ cup of wine or cooking sherry
½ envelope of dry onion soup mix

Mix all ingredients together in a baking dish and cover. Set crock-pot on "stew" setting or bake at 325 degrees for 3 hours.

DUNGENESS CRAB BURGER

1½ cups of Dungeness crabmeat pieces
2 hard-boiled eggs, chopped
4 cheddar cheese slices
3 ounces of mayonnaise
3 ounces of chili sauce
3 tablespoons of olives, chopped
Juice from ½ lemon
4 hamburger buns

Combine crabmeat with egg, mayonnaise, chili sauce, olives and lemon juice. Mix thoroughly. Spread mixture on split hamburger buns, place on a broiler pan and broil for 5 to 7 minutes. Top with a slice of cheddar cheese and return to broiler until cheese is melted.

EARLY KICK-OFF BREAKFAST SPAM

12 ounces of Spam
3 cups rice
8 eggs
Soy sauce

Cut Spam into ¼-inch slices. Brown both sides in skillet and set aside. Steam rice and set aside. Scramble 8 eggs in skillet. Put rice on plates, top with eggs and put Spam on the side. Sprinkle with soy sauce.

HONEY BARBECUED CHICKEN

3 pounds of chicken parts
3 tablespoons of honey
3 tablespoons of mustard
1 tablespoon of sesame seeds

Barbecue the chicken on the grill. Mix honey, mustard and sesame seeds together in a small bowl. Ten minutes before serving, brush the sauce on the hot chicken pieces.

MAN CAVE CHICKEN

3 ounces of sliced, dried
3 large chicken breasts, boneless and skinless
6 slices of bacon
1 can of condensed cream of mushroom soup
1 cup of sour cream

Run cold water over beef, drain and place in a large baking dish. Cut chicken breasts in half, put them on the beef and cover with bacon. Bake at 350 degrees for 30 minutes. Mix soup and sour cream together and pour over chicken. Bake for an additional 25 minutes.

P.A.T. CHICKEN

3 frozen, skinless chicken breasts
  (or 6 halves)
1 package of onion soup mix
1 can of cranberry sauce jelly

Place the frozen chicken in a crock-pot. Pour dry soup mix and cranberry sauce on top. Put on lid and bake on medium heat for 3½ hours.

POOR MAN'S STEAK

2 pounds of hamburger
1 cup of cracker crumbs
1 cup of milk
1 teaspoon of salt
¼ teaspoon of pepper
1 chopped onion
Flour
Oil (or butter)
1 cup of mushroom soup

Mix all ingredients together, except flour and oil in the shape of a loaf. Chill overnight. Cut into slices and dip into flour then brown on both sides in a skillet. Place in a roasting pan or baking dish and cover with the mushroom soup and a little water. Bake at 350 degrees for 90 minutes.

SEATTLE HASH

2 cups of ham, chopped or diced
2 cups of chopped cooked potatoes
1½ onions, minced
2 tablespoons parsley
1 cup of milk
Salt and pepper
Oil or lard

Mix all ingredients except milk. Place oil or lard in a skillet over medium heat. When hot, spread hash mix evenly in skillet. Brown the bottom of the hash quickly, 10 to 15 minutes. Add milk and mix. Cover cook slowly until crisp, about 10 minutes.

WILD, WILD TURKEY

1 large turkey, quartered
4 tablespoons of honey
1 teaspoon of parsley
½ cup of chopped onion
1 cup of white wine
1 cup of chicken stock
Butter
Salt and pepper

Brush turkey with honey and season with salt and pepper to taste. Place the turkey in a baking pan. Bake at 450 degrees for 30 minutes basting often with butter. Mix onion, chicken stock, win and parsley together. Pour over turkey. Cover and bake at 250 degrees for 1 hour or until turkey is done. Baste turkey occasionally with pan drippings.

PIZZA

AUSTRALIAN RULES PIZZA
(It's Upside Down)

2 pounds of ground meat
1 package of Pillsbury crescent rolls
1 package of Italian spaghetti sauce mix
2 cups of mozzarella cheese, grated
1 cup of onion, chopped
16 ounces of tomato sauce
8 ounces of sour cream

Brown meat and add in onions, tomato sauce and spaghetti sauce mix. Simmer until onions are tender. Grease the bottom of a baking dish. Pour in meat mixture. Layer, in order, sour cream, grated cheese and crescent roll dough. Bake the pizza 350 degrees for 20 minutes or until rolls are brown.

EXTRA MAN ON THE FIELD PIZZA ROLLS

2 cans of refrigerated pizza crust
Garlic salt
Italian seasoning
Flour
1 cup of diced pepperoni
1 cup of shredded cheese of choice
½ cup of Parmesan cheese
1 jar of pizza or spaghetti sauce

Dust wax paper or cutting board with flour and roll out pizza crust. Season each crust with the Italian seasoning and garlic salt. Top with cheese and meat. Roll the crust into a tight log. Slice into pizza-roll sized pieces. Place on a lightly greased baking sheet. Bake at 425 degrees for 10 to 12 minutes. Serve with sauce for dipping.

PIZZA DOGS

4 hot dogs
4 hot dog buns, split
½ cup of marinara sauce
4 ounces of mozzarella, shredded
¼ cup of diced pepperoni

Cook the hot dogs on grill or in a skillet for 5 to 8 minutes, according to the package directions. Place a hot dog in each bun and, dividing evenly, top with the warmed marinara, pepperoni and mozzarella. Grill, bake or broil until the mozzarella has melted and browned, about 2 minutes.

PIZZA GRILLED CHEESE SANDWICH

8 slices of bread
¾ cup pizza sauce
8 slices of mozzarella
24 slices of pepperoni
2 tablespoons Crisco
Toppings of choice

Spread 1 teaspoon of sauce on each piece of bread. Place a slice of cheese on 4 bread slices and 6 slices of pepperoni. Add other four slices of cheese and bread. Melt 1 tablespoon of Crisco in skillet on medium heat and add sandwiches. Grill 2 to 4 minutes until golden brown. Add remaining Crisco, let melt and turn sandwiches to grill other side.

PIZZA TURNOVER...ON THE GOAL LINE

2 packages of refrigerator crescent rolls
Pepperoni (either diced or mini-slices)
Mozzarella cheese (shredded)
Pizza sauce

Place pepperoni and cheese inside roll with a teaspoon of sauce. Seal the edges well. Bake at 375 degrees for 10 to 12 minutes.

SPRING GAME PIZZA

Ritz Crackers or Triscuit Crackers
Slices of cheese cut into eighths
Tomato Sauce
Pepperoni slices

Lay crackers on a cookie sheet. Layer with cheese, sauce and pepperoni. Bake at 350 degrees for 3 to 5 minutes.

TIME-OUT PIZZA

1 jar of tomato sauce
1 Package of shredded mozzarella cheese
1 Package of pepperoni
Bagels, bread or hamburger buns

Spread sauce on your bread of choice. Top with cheese and pepperoni. Bake in pre-heated oven or toaster oven for 2 to 5 minutes. Keep an eye on it or you'll need the fire extinguisher.

SALADS

COLE SLAW SALAD

1 purple cabbage
1 green cabbage
1 cup of cheese
1 cup bologna, diced (ring bologna works)
1 red onion, sliced into rings
1 green pepper
Salt, pepper and garlic salt (optional)
French dressing (optional)

Finely cut cabbages, cheese, bologna onion and pepper. Toss in tomato as an option. Add seasonings to taste. Once these are all tossed together, refrigerate at least 8 hours and serve cold with dressing of choice.

FRUIT SALAD

1 orange
1 apple
1 banana
1 large can of pineapple chunks, in juice
½ cup of raisins
½ cup of dates

Peel, slice and chop orange, apple and banana. Mix ingredients in a large bowl.

MACARONI SALAD

2 cups of cooked macaroni
1 cup of cheese, finely diced or shredded
½ cup stuffed olives, sliced (optional)
½ cup diced celery
1 small onion, diced
2 hard-boiled eggs, diced
Mayonnaise and salt

Mix all of the ingredients together and get ready for the kick-off.

PASTA SALAD

1 package of tri-colored pasta
1 small bottle of Italian dressing
1 package of Italian dressing mix
1 cucumber, sliced
1 cup of cherry tomatoes
1 can of large olives (6 ounces)
1 avocado, diced

Cook pasta, drain and rinse in cold water. Add dry dressing, cucumber, tomatoes and avocado to the pasta. Stir in ½ bottle of dressing and add olives.

PEPPERONI SALAD

1 head of lettuce
2 tomatoes
4 ounces of mozzarella cheese, diced
1 cup of garbanzo beans
½ cup of pepperoni, diced
¼ cup of green onion, diced
½ cup of Italian dressing
Salt and pepper to taste

Chop or shred lettuce in to pieces. Slice tomatoes into chunks. Combine all of the ingredients and toss lightly.

SNICKERS SALAD

1 carton of Cool Whip
4 Snickers bars in pieces
2 red apples sliced
1 green apple sliced

Freeze candy bars and slam on counter or hit with a hammer to break into pieces. Combine everything in a bowl and mix well. Chill and serve.

TACO SALAD

1 head of lettuce
1 red onion, chopped
2 cups of kidney beans, drained
½ pound of cheddar cheese, shredded
2 tomatoes, chopped
1 avocado, diced
1 can of olives, chopped
16 ounces of 1000 Island dressing
1 bag of corn chips, crushed
    (You don't have to use the plain variety)

Mix all ingredients in a large bowl adding hot hamburger last. Toss with dressing.

TUNA SEASON SALAD

2 cans of tuna, drained
4 hard-boiled eggs, chopped
1 small onion, chopped
4 pickles, diced
1½ cups of mayonnaise
2 tablespoons of pickle juice

Combine all ingredients thoroughly. Chill in the refrigerator for at least 3 hours.

THREE BEAN SALAD

1 can of kidney beans
1 can of garbanzo beans
1 can of green beans
1 small red onion, chopped
½ cup of Italian dressing

Mix ingredients and refrigerate for at least 4 hours.

WEST COAST SEA FOAM SALAD

28 ounces of canned pears
6 ounces of cream cheese, softened
3 ounce package of lime Jell-O
2 ½ cups of whipped topping

Drain pears. Bring 1 cup of the pear juice to a boil and dissolve Jell-O in it. Mash pears thoroughly and combine with cream cheese. Now mix in the Jell-O juice. Let rest until slightly thickened. Fold in whipped topping and chill in the refrigerator for 3 hours.

SANDWICHES & BREADS

BEER BOMB HOT ROLLS

3 cups of Bisquick
3 tablespoons of sugar
12 ounces of beer

Mix well. Fill muffin tins two-thirds full. Bake at 350 degrees until brown.

BEER CHEESE MUFFINS

2 cups Bisquick
2 tablespoons sugar
1 cup of beer
4 ounces of shredded cheddar cheese

Mix ingredients and fill greased muffin cup 2/3 full with the batter. Let stand for 12 minutes and bake at 375 degrees for 15 minutes. Makes 12 muffins.

BREWSKI BREAD

3 cups of self-rising flour
3 tablespoons of sugar
¼ teaspoon of salt
12 ounces of beer

Mix together all four ingredients thoroughly. Pour into a greased loaf pan. Bake at 350 degrees for 40 to 45 minutes.

BUTTERSCOTCH ROLLS

2 loaves frozen bread dough
1 box butterscotch pudding mix
1 cup of brown sugar
½ cup milk
½ cup melted butter
1 teaspoon of cinnamon
1 teaspoon of vanilla

Thaw bread dough and cut into cubes. Place in a 9-inch by 13-inch pan or Bundt pan. Mix remaining ingredients and pour over cubes. Let rise until it doubles in size. Bake at 350 degrees for 30 minutes.

CHAMPIONSHIP GRILLED CHEESE SANDWICH

3 ounces of softened cream cheese
¾ cup mayonnaise
1 cup shredded cheddar cheese
1 cup shredded mozzarella cheese
½ teaspoon garlic powder
1/8 teaspoon seasoning salt
10 slices of Italian bread (½ inch thick)
2 tablespoons butter

In a bowl, mix cream cheese and mayonnaise until smooth. Stir in cheese, garlic powder and seasoning salt. Spread 5 slices of bread with cheese mixture and top with remaining bread. Butter outside of sandwich and toast in a large pan or skillet for about 4 minutes a side or until golden brown.

GOBBLED UP SANDWICHES

4 turkey breast fillets
4 hoagie buns
1 cup of soy sauce
1 cup of Sprite
1 cup of cooking oil

Combine soy sauce, Sprite and oil. Marinate fillets overnight. Grill the meat 6 to 8 minutes per side until browned. Baste with the marinade while cooking.

ORCHARD GRILLED CHEESE SANDWICH

Sour Dough Bread (or your favorite)
Butter or Margarine
Sliced Sharp Cheddar
Sliced Havarti
Mayonnaise
Creamy Horse Radish Sauce
Bacon Bits
French's French Fried Onions
Pear Jam or Preserves
(peach or apricot work too)

For each sandwich butter one side of each slice of bread. On the other, spread one with a mixture of mayonnaise and horseradish sauce and one with the pear jam. Then between the 2 slices, add a slice of each cheese, bacon bits and French fried onions. Close and fry in pan until golden brown and cheese has melted.

REUBEN SLIDERS

1½ cups of corned beef, chopped
1 cup of sauerkraut
½ cup of shredded Swiss cheese
½ cup of Thousand Island dressing
1 loaf of thin-sliced cocktail rye

In a bowl combine corned beef, drained sauerkraut, shredded Swiss cheese and Thousand Island dressing. Mix well. Place mini-sandwiches on a baking sheet and bake at 375 degrees for 10 to 12 minutes or until cheese is melted.

SPICY BBQ PORK SANDWICHES

1½ cups of spicy ketchup
    (or blend ketchup and hot sauce)
½ cup of onion, finely diced
¼ cup of green onion, finely diced
1 tablespoon of brown sugar
1 teaspoon of salt
1½ teaspoons of dry mustard
3½ cups of pork, cooked and shredded
Tabasco sauce to taste
Hamburger buns

Combine ketchup, onion, pepper, brown sugar, salt, mustard and Tabasco sauce in a pan. Cover and simmer for 15 minutes. Now add pork to sauce, cover and simmer for 10 minutes. Serve the mixture on toasted buns.

For information on Tim Murphy's entire series
of "Cookbooks for Guys" visit
www.flanneljohn.com

44261730R00092

Made in the USA
San Bernardino, CA
10 January 2017